The Usborne
Little
Encyclopedia
of
Science

Rachel Firth

Designed by Helen Wood

Illustrated by David Hancock

Edited by Felicity Brooks and Anna Claybourne

Consultants: Sinclair MacLeod and Michael J. Reiss
Managing designer: Mary Cartwright
Digital manipulation: Michael Wheatley

Using Internet links

Throughout this book we have suggested interesting websites where you can find out more about science. To visit the sites, go to the Usborne Quicklinks Website at **www.usborne-quicklinks.com** and type the keywords "little science". Here are some of the things you can do on the websites:

• Build your own virtual rollercoaster

• Trick your brain with optical illusions

• Learn about the forces in toys

• Experiment online with magnets

Internet safety

When using the Internet, please make sure you follow these guidelines:

• Ask your parent's or guardian's permission before you connect to the Internet.

• If you write a message in a website guest book or on a website message board, do not include any personal information such as your full name, address or telephone number, and ask an adult before you give your email address.

• Never arrange to meet anyone you have talked to on the Internet.

• If a website asks you to log in or register by typing your name or email address, ask permission from an adult first.

• If you do receive an email from someone you don't know, tell an adult and do not reply to the email.

Site availability

The links in Usborne Quicklinks are regularly reviewed and updated, but occasionally, you may get a message that a site is unavailable. This might be temporary, so try again later, or even the next day. Websites do occasionally close down and when this happens, we will replace them with new links in Usborne Quicklinks. Sometimes we add extra links too, if we think they are useful. So when you visit Usborne Quicklinks, the links may be slightly different from those described in your book.

Downloadable pictures

Pictures in this book marked with a ★ symbol can be downloaded from Usborne Quicklinks for your own personal use, for example, to illustrate a homework report or project. The pictures are the copyright of Usborne Publishing and may not be used for any commercial or profit-related purpose. To download a picture, go to Usborne Quicklinks and follow the instructions there.

Notes for parents and guardians

The websites described in this book are regularly reviewed and the links in Usborne Quicklinks are updated. However, the content of a website may change at any time and Usborne Publishing is not responsible for the content on any website other than its own. We recommend that children are supervised while on the Internet, that they do not use Internet chat rooms, and that you use Internet filtering software to block unsuitable material. Please ensure that your children read and follow the safety guidelines printed on the left. For more information, see the "Net Help" area on the Usborne Quicklinks Website.

To go to all the websites described in this book, go to **www.usborne-quicklinks.com** and enter the keywords "little science".

Computer not essential

If you don't have access to the Internet, don't worry. This book is a complete, self-contained reference book on its own.

Contents

A slug uses its strong
stomach muscle to
crawl up a plant stem.

What is science?

Science is what we know about the world around us. Why do volcanoes erupt? What is gravity? Is there life on other planets? How do our brains work? Science tries to answer all these questions and many more.

Being a scientist

People who do science are called scientists. They study things by looking at them closely, asking questions, and doing experiments to find out how they work.

Scientists who study animals, such as this macaw, are called zoologists.

Scientists have found out why leaves turn red or brown in the autumn.

Scientists can use their scientific knowledge to help them invent things, like this mobile phone.

Internet link

For a link to a website where you can find out about some of the useful things scientists have invented, go to **www.usborne-quicklinks.com**

Studies of macaws have shown that their bright feathers may help them to find a mate.

Scientists have found 17 different species (types) of macaws in the wild.

4

Branches of science

There are hundreds of different kinds, or branches, of science, and many different kinds of scientists. Here are just a few of them.

Biologists study living things.

Botanists study just plants.

Chemists study chemicals.

Technology

Scientists can use their understanding of the world to design or invent new things. Without science, we wouldn't have many of the machines and medicines we have today. Using science in this way is called technology.

Medical scientists use X-ray machines to look inside people's bodies. The picture above is an X-ray photo of a foot. Can you see the bones?

This is a machine called a robot. It can move around and make its own simple decisions.

Some types of robots can do dangerous jobs instead of humans.

What scientists do

To find out about things, scientists do experiments. These are tests that show how living things, objects or substances behave.

Internet link

For a link to a website where you'll find lots of fun science experiments to try out, go to **www.usborne-quicklinks.com**

Asking questions

Scientists use experiments to help them answer questions. For example, a scientist might ask, "does music make plants grow faster?"

As an experiment, she could take two groups of plants and play music to just one of them, to see which grew faster.

These pictures show a simple experiment on plants.

A scientist grows two similar groups of plants.

Music is played to only one of the groups.

Later, the two groups can be compared.

Theories

Scientists think up theories that might explain how things work. For example, they might have a theory that penguins travel to a certain area because there is more food there. Then they do experiments to test their theories.

Scientists write down their results and repeat their experiments to make sure they work.

—— Transmitter

This penguin is part of an experiment. Scientists have fitted it with a jacket containing a transmitter. (It doesn't hurt the penguin at all.)

The transmitter will send signals that the scientists can collect. From this, they can track the penguin's movements.

Observing

Observing means watching and measuring things very carefully. It's an important part of being a scientist.

Scientists often use tools to help them observe things. For example, astronomers (space scientists) use powerful telescopes to study planets, stars and galaxies.

Telescopes make far away things look nearer. There is a huge telescope in this building that a team of astronomers uses to watch the night sky.

This is a comet. Comets are balls of ice and dust that zoom through space. By observing the path of a comet, astronomers can work out where it will go next.

Do your own experiment

Find out if adding salt to water will make a difference to how things float in it. You will need:
2 half-full glasses of water; 2 fresh eggs; 10 heaped teaspoons of salt

1. Stir the salt into one glass of water until it has dissolved and is invisible.

2. Put an egg in each glass. Do both eggs float? Do they both behave the same way?

You can find out more about floating on pages 46-47.

Our Universe

The Universe is the name for space and everything in it, including stars, planets, and our own planet, the Earth. Scientists are always working to find out more about the Universe.

This is the planet Jupiter. It is 11 times wider than the Earth.

Stars and planets

The Universe contains billions of stars. They look small because they are very far away. In fact, each star is a giant ball of burning gas. Some stars have balls of rock, called planets, orbiting (circling) around them.

The Big Dipper   Orion

The patterns stars form in the sky are known as constellations. Here are two of them.

Galaxies

In space, stars and planets form huge groups called galaxies. Our planet, the Earth, and our nearest star, the Sun, are part of a galaxy called the Milky Way.

Although it's just a small part of the Universe, the Milky Way is enormous. The world's fastest plane would take about two million million million years to fly across it.

This is the Milky Way. Scientists think that there are about 200 billion stars in it.

Our Solar System

The Sun is a star. It has nine planets, including Earth, orbiting around it. Together, the Sun and its planets are known as the Solar System.

Internet link

For a link to a website where you can find out more about the planets in our Solar System and do a quiz about them, go to **www.usborne-quicklinks.com**

This picture shows the nine planets in the Solar System, and how big they are compared to each other.

Pluto

Neptune   Uranus

Saturn

Jupiter

Mars   Venus

Earth   Mercury

The Earth and Moon

The Earth is the third planet from the Sun. It is the only planet we know where people, animals and plants live.

A smaller ball of rock called the Moon orbits around the Earth. Some other planets have moons too. For example, Saturn has over 30.

This is what part of the Earth looks like from space. The blue areas are the seas and oceans.

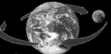

The red arrows show the path the Moon takes as it orbits around the Earth.

Astronauts (people who travel in space) have visited our Moon six times. This photo shows an astronaut on the Moon.

What is the Earth made of?

Our planet, the Earth, is a huge ball of rock and metal. We live on its crust, or hard surface. Inside the Earth is so hot that some of the rock and metal there is molten, or melted.

Inside the Earth

Scientists think the Earth is made up of layers, with a round metal core in the middle. In this picture, the Earth has been cut open to show the layers inside.

Crust made of solid rock

Mantle made of partly molten rock

Outer core made of molten metal

Inner core made of solid metal

Earthquakes and volcanoes

The Earth's crust is made up of huge pieces, called plates. They slide around very slowly. When they push against each other, we feel an earthquake. When a volcano erupts, magma, or molten rock, from inside the Earth bursts right out through the crust.

In a volcanic eruption, magma gushes out of the ground. Magma that has come to the Earth's surface is called lava.

Rocks and minerals

The Earth's crust contains many different types of rocks. They are made up of basic ingredients called minerals. Minerals include metals, such as gold and iron, and precious stones such as diamonds.

We use rocks and minerals for all sorts of things.

The salt we put on our food is a kind of mineral.

This building is made from a rock called marble.

Jewellery is often made of metal and precious stones.

This is a slice of a mineral called agate.

Internet link

For a link to a website where you can see an animation of a volcano erupting, go to **www.usborne-quicklinks.com**

Watery world

Less than a third of the Earth's surface is land. The rest is covered by seas and oceans. They are home to millions of kinds of fish and other animals.

Coral reefs are underwater structures made by tiny animals called corals. They are home to shellfish, octopuses, sharks and many other fish.

The seasons

In most places on Earth, the year is divided into four seasons. They are spring, summer, autumn and winter.

Changing seasons

The weather changes from season to season. It is coldest in winter and hottest in summer. Many plants also change with the seasons. You can tell what season it is by looking at some kinds of trees.

In the summer, trees like this one are covered in green leaves.

In the autumn, the leaves on the trees begin to turn red or brown and die.

In spring, as it gets warmer, new leaves start to grow on trees.

By winter, all the leaves have died and fallen off.

North and south

The two halves of the Earth are called the northern and southern hemispheres. When countries in the southern hemisphere have their winter, countries in the northern hemisphere have their summer.

The picture on the right shows the Earth's two hemispheres. The imaginary line around the middle is called the equator.

Internet link

For a link to a website where you can watch a cartoon and try a quiz about the seasons, go to **www.usborne-quicklinks.com**

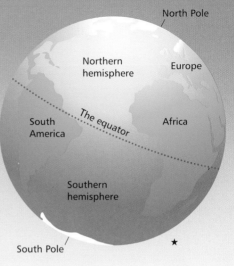

North Pole

Northern hemisphere

Europe

The equator

South America

Africa

Southern hemisphere

South Pole

★

What makes the seasons happen?

The Earth is tilted a little as it goes around the Sun. The hemisphere that is tilted toward the Sun gets more hot sunlight and it is summer there.

The hemisphere tilted away from the Sun has winter. Each year, first one half and then the other is nearer the Sun. This makes the seasons change.

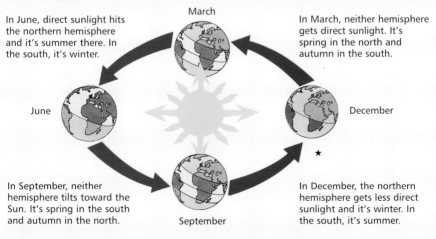

In June, direct sunlight hits the northern hemisphere and it's summer there. In the south, it's winter.

March

In March, neither hemisphere gets direct sunlight. It's spring in the north and autumn in the south.

June

December

In September, neither hemisphere tilts toward the Sun. It's spring in the south and autumn in the north.

September

In December, the northern hemisphere gets less direct sunlight and it's winter. In the south, it's summer.

★

Weather

There are lots of different kinds of weather. It can be rainy, snowy, sunny or windy. The three main things that make the weather happen are the Sun, the air and water.

The Sun gives out heat.

The air moves to make wind.

Water makes rain and snow.

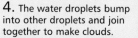

4. The water droplets bump into other droplets and join together to make clouds.

Rainy days

The amount of water in the world is always the same. Rain isn't new water. Follow the numbers to find out where rain comes from.

3. Up in the sky, it's cooler and the gas turns back into tiny water droplets.

5. As more water is added, the droplets get bigger and heavier and fall as rain.

2. The water turns into water vapour, a gas which we can't see, and rises up into the sky.

6. The rain falls down to the ground where it flows back into seas, lakes and rivers.

1. The Sun heats up the water in seas, lakes, rivers, and snow on mountain tops.

Windy weather

When it's windy, it's because the air is moving around. You can't see the wind, but you can see it blowing leaves around and feel it on your face.

A gentle wind is called a breeze. It can help dry wet clothes.

Gales are much stronger winds. They can blow tiles off roofs.

Hurricanes are very strong winds that can do a lot of damage.

Rainbows

Sometimes it rains even though the Sun is shining. Raindrops split sunlight into different colours. When this happens you might see a rainbow. From the ground, it usually looks like an arch, but from an aircraft, it may be a circle.

Icy snowflakes

Snowflakes are made when it gets so cold that the water in a cloud freezes and turns into ice. Snowflakes all have six sides or points, but they form millions of different patterns.

Every snowflake is a different shape.

Make a rainbow

You can make your own rainbow even when it's not raining, as long as the Sun is shining. You will need:

a plastic tray or bowl; a piece of paper; a mirror

1. Put the tray of water in a sunny place, such as on a windowsill, or outside.

2. Stand the mirror in the tray so the Sun can shine through the water onto the mirror.

3. Hold the paper above the tray. Tilt the mirror until you see a rainbow on the paper.

Internet link

For a link to a website where you can find out more about hurricanes and watch video clips of them, go to **www.usborne-quicklinks.com**

Living things

There are millions of living things on planet Earth. These include plants, animals and people. All living things share certain features.

Living things need a gas called oxygen. A fish gets oxygen from the water it takes in through its mouth.

Air and food

To stay alive, most living things need a gas called oxygen. They also need food. Plants make their own food using energy from the Sun. Animals get energy by eating plants or other animals.

A buttercup plant uses energy from sunlight to grow.

A snail gets its energy from eating the buttercup.

A thrush eats the snail, and gains its energy.

New life and growth

Living things can make new living things. These live on after their parents have died. Animals make babies, and plants produce new plants. As they get older, most living things grow and change.

These baby penguins look like small versions of their parents.

Some animals give birth to live babies. Penguins, like other birds, lay eggs with the babies inside.

Internet link

For a link to a website where you can find out about all the different types of living things, go to **www.usborne-quicklinks.com**

Moving

All living things can move. Most animals can move from one place to another. Plants can only move parts of themselves, and they usually move too slowly for you to see.

Some animals, such as this cheetah, can move at very high speeds.

Sensitivity

Living things are sensitive to changes in the world around them, such as changes of light or heat. Animals usually react to these changes more quickly than plants.

A sunflower slowly turns so the flower always faces the Sun.

When a fly touches sensitive hairs on the leaves of a Venus flytrap, the leaves snap shut and trap the fly.

Waste

Plants and animals produce stuff inside them that they don't need. They all have ways of getting rid of the waste.

Dung beetles eat the solid waste (dung) of other animals.

— Fly

Venus flytrap

17

Cells

All living things are made up of tiny units called cells. Most cells are much too small to see. Scientists have to look at them through microscopes.

> **Internet link**
> For a link to a website where you can find out more about cells, go to **www.usborne-quicklinks.com**

What is a cell?

A cell is a tiny structure with its own protective skin. Inside, a cell has even smaller parts called organelles. In many living things, such as humans, millions of cells stick together to make up body tissues such as skin, muscle and bone.

This picture shows human fat seen through a microscope. The pink blobs are cells.

Plant or animal?

Animal cells have a skin called a cell membrane. Inside, the parts of the cell float in a watery gel. Plant cells have a cell membrane and a tough cell wall that gives them a fixed shape.

Both plant and animal cells have a nucleus, which controls the cell.

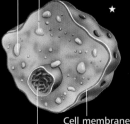

Organelles (cell parts)

Nucleus

Cell membrane (skin)

Nucleus

This picture shows an animal cell, cut in half so you can see inside it.

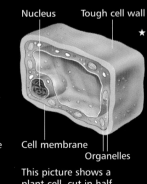

Nucleus   Tough cell wall

Cell membrane

Organelles

This picture shows a plant cell, cut in half so you can see inside it.

Single-celled creatures

Some very small living things have only one cell. There are single-celled animals called amoebas, and single-celled plants called algae.

Bacteria also have only one cell each. They are not plants or animals, but belong in a group of their own.

Bacteria are all around us. Most are harmless, but some, like these salmonella bacteria, can make you sick.

Bacteria are extremely tiny. This photograph was taken using a very powerful microscope.

Looking at cells

Microscopes make things look bigger. When microscopes were invented, over 300 years ago, scientists could begin to look very closely at living things, and cells were discovered.

Today, powerful electron microscopes like this one help scientists to look deep inside cells.

Plants

Plants are living things that can make their own food using energy from the Sun. Scientists have found more than 250,000 species, or types, of plants.

How plants make food

Plants make food inside their leaves. To do this, they mix water from the soil with a gas from the air called carbon dioxide.

To turn these things into food, plants use light energy from the Sun. This process is called photosynthesis (say "foe-toe-*sin*-thuh-sis").

Roots in the soil

Most plants have roots. Roots reach into the soil, holding the plant in place. They also suck up water and chemicals. Plants need water to make food and to keep their cells healthy.

Without enough water, most plants quickly droop.

They will recover if they are watered soon enough.

Sun

Plants need light to help them make food and stay alive.

Photosynthesis happens in cells inside a plant's leaves.

Most plants have a central stem.

Roots branch out into the soil to reach as much water as possible.

Plants and seeds

Like all living things, plants reproduce, or have babies. To do this, they make seeds that can grow into new plants. The flower is the part of a plant that makes seeds.

Internet link

For a link to a website where you can go on an adventure to solve the mysteries of how plants work, go to **www.usborne-quicklinks.com**

Poppy
seedhead

★
When the petals drop off the flower, seeds are released from the seedhead.

★
Some types of seeds, such as dandelion seeds, are blown away on the wind.

★
Other types of seeds are eaten by animals and dropped far away in their droppings.

★
If a seed lands in soil, with enough water and sunshine, it can grow into a new plant.

Plant protection

Most plants stay in one place, so they're in danger of being eaten by animals. To protect themselves, many plants have sharp thorns, stinging hairs or poisonous leaves or berries.

This cactus's thorns protect it from most types of animals.

Grow your own bean plant

You will need:

a glass jar; paper towels; kidney beans; a pot; some compost or soil

1. Line a glass jar with paper towels and keep them damp with water.

2. Put dried kidney beans (a type of seed) between the glass and the paper.

3. Each day look for shoots growing up and little roots growing down.

4. To grow the plants further, plant each bean in a pot of compost and water it.

Animals

Animals are the biggest group of living things. They live all over our planet. Humans are animals too.

Finding food

Unlike plants, animals can move around to look for food. Animals that eat plants are called herbivores. Animals that hunt and eat other animals are called carnivores.

 ★

Squirrels are herbivores. They eat nuts.

 ★

Chameleons are carnivores. They catch flies.

 ★

Badgers eat both plants and animals.

This bald eagle has caught a fish to eat.

Having babies

Most animals can have babies. The babies grow inside their mother's body or inside an egg she has laid.

When babies are big enough, they are born or hatch out of their eggs. This is a crocodile hatching.

Internet link

For a link to a website where you can explore the world of animals, go to **www.usborne-quicklinks.com**

Did you know?

• More than a million different species, or types, of animals have been found so far.

• The biggest animal, the blue whale, can be 33m (100ft) long – as long as 3 buses.

Animal homes

The places where animals and plants live are called habitats. Over time, different species slowly change, or adapt, to suit their habitats.

Safe places

Many animal species are in danger of dying out. This can happen if we destroy wild habitats to make space for farms and towns. Reserves are places where habitats are protected, and animals can live safely.

These animals live in North America, in a hot, wet habitat called a swamp.

Woodpeckers live in woods. They eat insects that live in bark.

Zebra butterflies get their food from flowers.

Green tree frogs have suckers on their feet to climb slippery branches.

Otters are equally at home on dry land or in water.

Cottonmouth snakes live in places where there is long grass. They are also good swimmers.

Terrapins swim under water, but come to the surface to breathe.

Gambusia fish eat mosquito eggs that float on the water surface.

Alligators spend a lot of time in water, where they hunt fish and other animals.

Your body

Have you ever wondered what's inside you? Your body is made up of lots of separate parts. They all do different jobs to help you stay alive.

Organs

Organs are important body parts such as the heart, lungs, stomach and brain. Most of them are in the upper body and head. You can see some of the main organs in this picture.

Each organ has a special job to do. For example, your stomach holds the food you eat, and your lungs take air into your body.

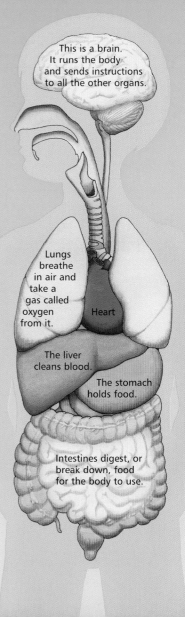

This is a brain. It runs the body and sends instructions to all the other organs.

Lungs breathe in air and take a gas called oxygen from it.

Heart

The liver cleans blood.

The stomach holds food.

Intestines digest, or break down, food for the body to use.

How much air do your lungs hold?

You will need: a plastic bottle with a lid; a bendy straw; a bowl of water

★ **1.** Fill the bottle with water and put the lid on. Hold it upside down in the bowl and take off the lid.

2. Push the straw into the neck of the bottle. Breathe in deeply, then blow gently into the straw until your lungs are empty.

★ All the air you breathe out will be trapped at the top of the bottle. This is how much air your lungs can hold.

Blood

As well as organs, a human body contains up to five litres (nine pints) of blood. The heart pumps blood around the body along thousands of tubes called blood vessels. As it flows along, blood delivers oxygen and food to every part of the body.

Blood is made of cells (see page 18) floating in a liquid called plasma. This picture shows different types of blood cells.

Platelet (part of a blood cell)

White blood cell

Red blood cell

Feel your pulse

To feel your blood being pumped around your body, press two fingers on the inside of your wrist. The beating you feel is called your pulse.

★

Internet link

For a link to a website where you can discover some amazing heart and lung facts and see short movies of blood flowing around your body, go to **www.usborne-quicklinks.com**

Safe in your skin

Your skin gives your whole body a waterproof covering, and protects your insides from dirt and germs. Skin is made up of two main layers.

This close-up photograph shows the layers in human skin.

Hair

The top layer of skin is called the epidermis.

Underneath the epidermis is a thicker layer called the dermis.

Hair shaft

Hair root

Hair follicle

In some places, the epidermis reaches deep into the dermis and forms a hair follicle. A hair can grow out of each follicle.

Bones and muscles

Bones and muscles are
your body's support system.
They hold you up and let
you move around. Without
them, you'd be nothing
but a helpless blob.

Your skeleton

Together, your bones make up your
skeleton, which acts as a framework
for your whole body. Bendy joints
where bones meet let you move
into different positions.

Bones protect your
insides too. For example,
rib bones in your chest
stop the organs inside
from getting squashed.

Soft skeletons

A baby's bones are partly made of a
bendy material called cartilage. As the
baby grows, most of the cartilage
slowly turns into hard bone.

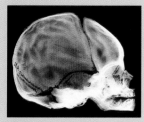

This is an X-ray
picture of a
newborn
baby's skull.
As the baby
grows, the
gaps in its
skull close
up and the
skull hardens.

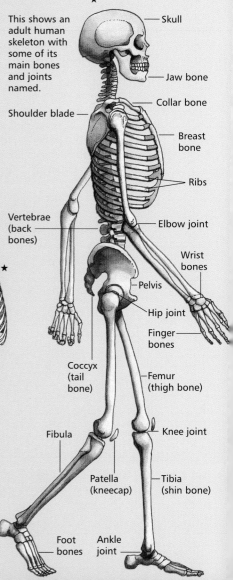

This shows an
adult human
skeleton with
some of its
main bones
and joints
named.

Skull

Jaw bone

Collar bone

Shoulder blade

Breast bone

Ribs

Vertebrae (back bones)

Elbow joint

Wrist bones

Lungs

Heart

Pelvis

Hip joint

Finger bones

Coccyx (tail bone)

Femur (thigh bone)

Knee joint

Fibula

Patella (kneecap)

Tibia (shin bone)

Foot bones

Ankle joint

Muscles

The bones of your skeleton are moved by muscles. These help you move in all kinds of ways, from walking or swimming to playing the recorder or using a computer.

You also have other muscles (in your heart, for example) that work without you even thinking about them.

> **Internet link**
>
> For a link to a website with online activities about bones, joints and muscles, go to **www.usborne-quicklinks.com**

There are over 600 muscles in the human body. This picture shows some of the main ones.

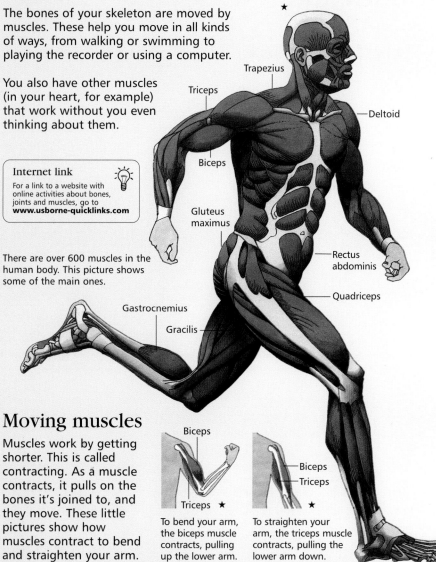

Trapezius

Triceps

Biceps

Deltoid

Gluteus maximus

Rectus abdominis

Quadriceps

Gastrocnemius

Gracilis

Moving muscles

Muscles work by getting shorter. This is called contracting. As a muscle contracts, it pulls on the bones it's joined to, and they move. These little pictures show how muscles contract to bend and straighten your arm.

Biceps

Triceps ★

To bend your arm, the biceps muscle contracts, pulling up the lower arm.

Biceps

Triceps

★

To straighten your arm, the triceps muscle contracts, pulling the lower arm down.

27

What happens to food?

The food you eat gives you the energy you need to live. But to get this energy, you have to turn food into chemicals in your body. This is called digestion.

Your food's journey

As food travels into and through your body, it gets turned into smaller and smaller bits. Follow the steps on the big picture to find out how this happens.

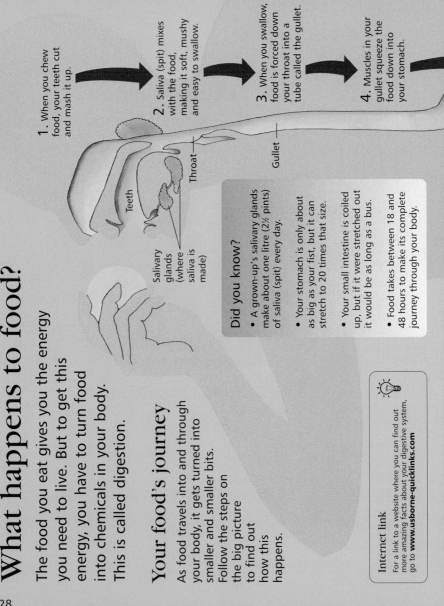

Teeth

Salivary glands (where saliva is made)

Throat

Gullet

1. When you chew food, your teeth cut and mash it up.

2. Saliva (spit) mixes with the food, making it soft, mushy and easy to swallow.

3. When you swallow, food is forced down your throat into a tube called the gullet.

4. Muscles in your gullet squeeze the food down into your stomach.

Did you know?

- A grown-up's salivary glands make about one litre (2½ pints) of saliva (spit) every day.

- Your stomach is only about as big as your fist, but it can stretch to 20 times that size.

- Your small intestine is coiled up, but if it were stretched out it would be as long as a bus.

- Food takes between 18 and 48 hours to make its complete journey through your body.

Internet link

For a link to a website where you can find out more amazing facts about your digestive system, go to www.usborne-quicklinks.com

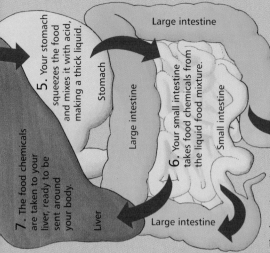

Large intestine

5. Your stomach squeezes the food and mixes it with acid, making a thick liquid.

Stomach

Large intestine

6. Your small intestine takes food chemicals from the liquid food mixture.

Small intestine

Rectum

9. The lumps of waste from your large intestine are squeezed out of your rectum when you go to the toilet.

7. The food chemicals are taken to your liver, ready to be sent around your body.

Liver

Large intestine

8. The large intestine collects food that can't be digested. It takes water out of it, leaving lumps of waste called faeces.

Food for your cells

After food has been broken down into chemicals, it is carried all around your body in your blood. Some food is used to give your cells the energy they need to work – for example, to make muscles move. Some food is used to build new cells and repair injuries.

If you eat more food than you need, your body stores it as fat. This is why you get fatter if you eat a lot and don't exercise much.

Waste

Most food contains bits that can't be digested, such as pips and fruit skin. They go into your large intestine and collect into lumps, which end up in the toilet.

Millions of tiny bacteria, like these *E. coli* bacteria, live inside your intestines. They help themselves to your food, but are usually harmless.

Your brain and senses

Your brain controls your body. Your five senses – sight, hearing, touch, taste and smell – tell your brain what's going on around you, so it can make decisions.

This picture shows a signal (in green) jumping between two neurons in your brain.

Brain bundle

Your brain is made of a big bundle of cells called neurons. When you think, your neurons are passing signals to each other. Neurons also link your brain to your sense organs and to other parts of your body.

This scan of a person's head shows the brain inside the skull.

The skull, shown here in blue, protects your brain.

The brain is this blue and yellow area. The yellow lines are folds in the brain's surface.

The brain stem links your brain to your spinal cord and so to the rest of your body.

Seeing things

You see things because light bounces off them and goes into your eyes. Your eyes collect the light patterns and turn them into signals your brain can understand.

4. The optic nerve (made of neurons) carries signals to your brain.

1. Light bounces off an object.

2. The light enters your pupil, which is the black dot in the middle of your eye.

3. Patterns of light hit your retina, an area of light-sensitive cells on the inside of your eye.

Internet link 💡

For a link to a website where you can find some amazing facts about senses, go to **www.usborne-quicklinks.com**

How you hear

Sounds make tiny particles in the air vibrate (move to and fro). You hear when these vibrating particles hit your ears. The vibrations are turned into signals that are sent to your brain.

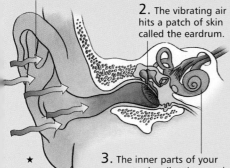

1. Sounds make vibrations travel through the air.

2. The vibrating air hits a patch of skin called the eardrum.

3. The inner parts of your ear sense the vibrations and send signals to your brain.

Taste and smell

Sensitive spots called taste buds on your tongue can detect a few simple tastes. Sensitive cells in your nose detect different smells, and also help you tell the difference between flavours.

Tiny pink bumps on your tongue have taste buds in them. The bumps are easier to see after a drink of milk.

Touch

There are millions of sensitive nerve endings in your skin. They can feel heat, cold, pressure and pain.

Some blind people use their fingers to read Braille writing, which is made up of tiny bumps.

31

Atoms and molecules

Everything is made out of tiny particles called atoms. Atoms can join together in groups called molecules.

Internet link

For a link to a website where you can play a game and find out about materials and molecules, go to **www.usborne-quicklinks.com**

What is an atom?

An atom is like a tiny ball. It has a centre, or nucleus, and outer layers called shells. There are about 100 types of atoms.

Atoms are so tiny that you can't see them. A piece of paper, such as this page, is about a million atoms thick.

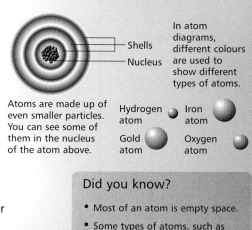

Shells
Nucleus

In atom diagrams, different colours are used to show different types of atoms.

Atoms are made up of even smaller particles. You can see some of them in the nucleus of the atom above.

Hydrogen atom

Iron atom

Gold atom

Oxygen atom

Making molecules

Atoms sometimes join together to make bigger units called molecules. This joining together is called bonding.

These pictures show two types of atoms bonding to make water molecules.

Did you know?

- Most of an atom is empty space.

- Some types of atoms, such as francium, do not exist naturally. They can only be made by scientists in a science lab.

- Atoms constantly move around, even in solids. They jiggle, vibrate and bump into each other.

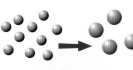

Hydrogen atoms

Oxygen atoms

Water molecules

Water

Water is made up of lots of water molecules.

Materials

All the things around us – rocks, air, water, sand, glass, wood, plastic, and even our bodies – are made of atoms and molecules. Scientists call all these different types of stuff "materials".

Sodium atoms + Chlorine atoms = Table salt molecules

Hydrogen atoms + Carbon atoms = Methane gas molecules

Molecules are often shown as balls (the atoms) and sticks (the bonds between them). This shows parts of two molecules of aspirin.

Materials hunt

Can you find things made of these materials in your home or classroom?

★ Paper
★ China
★ Plastic
★ Wood
★ Glass
★ Metal

Chemistry

Different materials behave in different ways. For example, if you heat butter, it melts, but if you heat an egg, it gets harder. Salt dissolves quickly in water, but sand doesn't.

Scientists called chemists study how materials behave, change, and bond together. This kind of science is called chemistry.

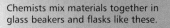

Chemists mix materials together in glass beakers and flasks like these.

Solids, liquids and gases

Most materials can exist in three different forms: solids, liquids and gases. In solids, molecules are packed together. In liquids and gases, they're more spread out.

Internet link

For a link to a website where you can find more examples of solids, liquids and gases, go to **www.usborne-quicklinks.com**

Solids

The molecules in solids are firmly attached to each other and don't move around much. Because of this, most solids stay the same shape.

Gold is a solid.

Molecules in solids are squashed tightly together.

Liquids

The molecules in liquids are not so squashed together. They can move around more and are not as firmly fixed to each other. This is why liquids can flow, splash and be poured.

Molecules in liquids are not squashed together.

Drinks are liquids. They flow into every part of a container.

Gases

The molecules in gases are not attached to each other at all and move around all the time at high speed. This means that gases quickly spread out to fill the space they are in. They have no shape of their own.

Gas molecules don't stick to each other at all.

Many gases are invisible. You can only see this gas because it is burning.

Make a gas

You can make carbon dioxide gas and blow up a balloon with it. You will need:

a narrow-necked jar; some baking soda; some vinegar; a balloon; a teaspoon

1. Fill a quarter of the jar with vinegar. Put the soda into the balloon, using the teaspoon.

★

2. Stretch the neck of the balloon over the top of the jar. Don't let any soda spill into the jar.

3. Quickly lift the balloon up to tip all of the soda into the jar. The vinegar will react with the soda, making bubbles.

★

When the vinegar and soda react (see page 37), they make carbon dioxide gas which fills the balloon, blowing it up a little.

Three forms

The same material can exist as a solid, a liquid or a gas. For example, water exists as a liquid, as solid ice, and as a gas called water vapour.

There is water vapour (water gas) in the air. As it cools, it forms clouds and may turn into rain.

Ice is frozen water. It is a solid.

Water in rivers and seas is a liquid.

How materials change

Materials can change all the time. They can grow, shrink and change between a solid, a liquid and a gas. They can also combine to make new materials.

Changing state

Materials can change between solid and liquid, or between liquid and gas. These changes are called changes of state. They often happen when materials heat up or cool down.

 ★ When juice gets very cold, it turns from a liquid to a solid. This is called freezing.

★ Wax turns from a solid into a liquid as a candle burns. This is called melting.

 ★ When you heat water, it turns from a liquid into a gas. This is called boiling.

★ When water vapour cools, it turns into a liquid – rain. This is called condensing.

Inside a freezer, it's cold enough for water to freeze into ice.

Getting bigger

Water expands (gets bigger) when it freezes. Most materials, however, shrink as they get colder and expand as they get hotter. For example, a thermometer* contains a liquid that expands as the temperature rises.

A thermometer contains !iquid in a narrow tube. (In this photo, the liquid is black.) As the liquid warms up, it gets bigger and fills more of the tube.

Make water get bigger

You will need:

a plastic bottle (don't use a glass bottle); a piece of foil; a freezer

1. Fill the bottle to the top with water. Cover the top with the foil.

2. Stand the bottle upright in the freezer. Leave it there overnight.

3. The water pushes the foil upwards as it freezes and gets bigger.

Mixing materials

Materials can be mixed together to make new materials. If you mix sand, cement, broken stones and water, you get concrete. Concrete is useful for building, because it is stronger than any of the ingredients by themselves.

Internet link

For a link to a website where you can find out how to make your own simple chemical reaction, go to **www.usborne-quicklinks.com**

The Catedral Metropolitana in Brazil is made of 16 curved concrete columns.

Reactions

In a mixture, materials are combined but their molecules do not change. Sometimes, however, materials react with each other. This means that when they are mixed, their molecules change and they turn into different materials.

Rusting happens to iron when it is left out in the rain or in damp air.

Molecules of iron react with oxygen atoms and water molecules.

The reaction makes a new type of molecule called iron oxide, or rust.

These rocks formed in Mono Lake in California, USA because of a reaction between two different chemicals in the lake.

Energy

Energy is the power that makes things happen. You can't see it, but it's all around you, making all kinds of objects move and work.

Electrical energy flows into lights and changes into heat and light energy.

All kinds of energy

Energy comes in many types, or "forms". For example, heat, light, electricity and sound are all forms of energy.

Internet link

For a link to a website where you can find out all kinds of things about energy, go to **www.usborne-quicklinks.com**

People shouting and machines moving release a lot of sound energy.

The same energy

You can't destroy or make energy. This means the amount of energy in the Universe is always the same. But one form of energy can change into another form.

Plants change light energy from the Sun into food energy.

Movement energy

Whenever something moves, it has energy. The energy of something that is moving is called kinetic energy.

At the top of the rollercoaster, the car contains stored energy.

To fly, these birds change energy stored in their bodies into kinetic energy.

As the car goes down the hill, stored energy changes into kinetic energy.

These flags have kinetic energy as they flutter in the breeze.

These children have a lot of kinetic energy because they are running fast.

Stored energy

Potential energy is energy that is stored, ready to use. When it's used, it turns into another form of energy, such as kinetic energy or heat.

As the hammer is lifted up, it gains a store of potential energy.

Food turns into stored energy in our bodies. A toffee apple will give this boy enough energy to walk for 20 minutes.

This boy's video camera uses electrical energy that's stored in a battery.

Forces

A force is a push or a pull that makes an object do something. For example, if you kick a ball, the force of your kick makes the ball move. Forces can also make things change their direction, speed and shape.

Direct forces

Some forces work by touching the object they are pushing or pulling on. These are called direct forces. Kicking a ball, lifting a pen or pulling your sock off are all examples of direct forces.

Pushing a toboggan is a direct force.

Pulling a toboggan uphill on a rope is a direct force.

From a distance

Some forces don't have to touch the things they work on. For example, gravity* pulls you down when you jump off a wall. A magnet pulls paperclips towards it. Scientists are still not sure how these distant forces work.

Forces can stop things too. This snowdrift has a force that has stopped this toboggan.

Gravity is a distant force. It is pulling the toboggans downhill, but not touching them.

Internet link
For a link to a website where you can find out about the forces in toys, go to **www.usborne-quicklinks.com**

*For more about gravity, see pages 44-45.

Balanced forces

When something isn't moving, you might think that there are no forces working on it. In fact, there are, but they are balanced against each other, and cancel each other out.

These two tug-of-war teams are not moving, because the forces they make are balanced. To win, one of the teams must use more force.

Using forces

We use forces all the time to move things, lift things and travel around. Machines help us to use forces to do things we can't do on our own. They turn our energy, or other forms of energy such as electricity, into the right kinds of force to do different jobs.

A digger turns electrical energy into a pulling force to scoop up a heavy load of soil.

Scissors are simple machines. Their sharp blades use the force of your fingers to cut things.

Hot and cold

Heat is a form of energy. Whenever you heat something up, you are giving it more energy.

Heating up

When many materials heat up, their molecules spread out. This makes them expand, or get bigger. When they cool down, they contract, or get smaller, again. As air heats up, it expands a lot, making it much lighter than cold air. This is why hot air balloons float.

The hot air inside these balloons is lighter than the air they float in. For more about floating, see pages 46-47.

Moving around

Heat moves from hotter to colder places. For example, hot food goes cold because its heat moves into the cooler air around it. You can't usually see heat, but it can be photographed with an infrared camera.

This picture was taken using an infrared camera. The red areas show where the buildings are giving out the most heat.

The Golden
Gate Bridge in
San Francisco, USA

Bridge gaps

Bridges often get slightly
longer as they heat up in the
sun. Large bridges have special
joints with gaps in them, so that
there's room for them to expand.

This is an expansion joint.
Joints like these allow
bridges to expand and
contract. Without them,
bridges could break and
collapse.

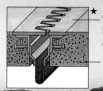

When a bridge expands in
hot weather, these plates
are pushed together.

Bridge

Expansion and contraction

You can do an experiment to see
how air expands when it is heated
and contracts when it cools down.
This is what you will need:

a bowl; a bottle; a balloon

1. Ask an adult to hold the
empty bottle under hot water
for a minute. Stretch the
balloon over its neck.

2. Half-fill the bowl with cold
water and stand the bottle in
it. The air cools and shrinks,
pulling the balloon inside.

3. Empty the bowl and ask
an adult to add hot water to
it. The expanding warm air
pushes the balloon out again.

Internet link

For a link to a website where you
can see fascinating infrared images
of objects and animals, go to
www.usborne-quicklinks.com

Measuring hotness

Temperature means how hot
something is. It is measured in
degrees Centigrade (°C) or
degrees Fahrenheit (°F).
Normal room temperature
is about 20°C (68°F).

Temperature is measured
using a thermometer.
Can you see what the
temperature is on
this thermometer?

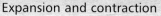

Gravity

When you jump up in the air, you drop back down again. This is because there's an invisible force pulling you down to the ground. This force is called gravity.

Mars

Pulling together

All objects have gravity and make a slight pull on other objects. With small objects, this force is too small to have an effect. But huge objects like planets have enough gravity to pull other things towards them.

Mercury

In empty space, far away from stars, planets and moons, there is hardly any gravity. This is why astronauts float.

Gravity on other planets

The bigger an object is, the stronger its gravity is. Very big planets, like Jupiter, have much stronger gravity than Earth. Small planets and moons have weaker gravity than Earth.

Jupiter's gravity is more than twice as strong as Earth's. If you could visit Jupiter, you wouldn't be able to move because its gravity is so strong.

Jupiter

Jupiter's moon Io is quite small and its gravity is much weaker than the Earth's. You could jump many times higher on Io than you can on Earth.

This is Io, one of Jupiter's many moons.

The Sun

Venus

The Earth is in orbit around the Sun.

The Moon is in orbit around the Earth.

Testing gravity

Gravity pulls objects at the same speed, even if they have different weights. Try testing this yourself. You will need:

tissue paper; a coin; two identical boxes (such as camera film boxes or food pots with lids)

1. Carefully tear a piece of tissue paper the same size as the coin. It will be lighter than the coin. ★

2. Drop the paper and the coin from the same height. The paper falls more slowly because air gets in its way. ★

3. Now put the coin in one box and the paper in the other. Put the lids on and drop both boxes together. ★

4. The boxes have the same air resistance and land at the same time, even though they are different weights. ★

Internet link

For a link to a website where you can find out how much you would weigh on planets which have more or less gravity than Earth, go to **www.usborne-quicklinks.com**

In orbit

In space, large objects orbit, or travel around, each other. Planets orbit the Sun. Moons orbit planets. This happens because of gravity.

Gravity doesn't pull planets and moons right together, because they're moving too fast. This diagram shows how orbits work.

Moon

Planet

Moons move very fast. A moon is always trying to fly away from its planet in a straight line.

Meanwhile, the planet's gravity pulls the moon towards it. The two forces balance out and the moon circles around the planet.

Floating

If you throw a stone into a pond, it will sink to the bottom. But if you put a balloon in some water, it will float. Why do some things float and others sink?

Weight and size

Floating is all about density – how heavy something is for its size. For example, a cork is light for its size. A piece of iron the same size as a cork is much heavier, because iron is denser than cork. Objects that are denser than water sink in water. Objects that are less dense than water float in water.

Internet link

For a link to a website where you can find out how to make a raisin float and sink in a fizzy drink, go to **www.usborne-quicklinks.com**

These inflatable rings are light for their size and float well.

If you try to push an inflatable ring under water, you'll feel the water pushing back.

Upthrust

Things float because water pushes up on them more than they push down. This upward force is called upthrust. If an object is denser than water, the water cannot provide enough upthrust, so the object sinks.

Does it float?

Guess which things will float in water and then see if you were right. You will need:

a bowl of water; solid things, such as a cork, a candle, a coin, an apple, a raisin, a plastic toy, an eraser.

1. Make a chart to compare your guesses with what actually happens.

2. Try floating different objects and write down which of them really float.

Will it float?		
	Guess	Actual
Cork	✓	☐
Coin	✓	☐
Candle	✗	☐
Apple	✗	☐

46

How do ships float?

Some ships are so huge, it seems amazing that they float – but they do. Even if a ship is made of heavy iron, it has a lot of air inside it. This makes the ship less dense than water, so it floats.

This big cruise ship is light for its size because it has lots of air inside it.

Floating in air

Floating in air is just like floating in water. Anything that is less dense than air will float in it. But because air is very light itself, not many other things are light enough to float in it.

This floating red buoy is used to warn boats that this stretch of water is dangerous.

These balloons are filled with a gas that's less dense than air. It makes them float.

People are almost the same density as water, and only just float. Air-filled life belts can help people to float better.

Salty sea

Salty water is denser than pure water. This makes it easier for people to float in it. A lake in Israel called the Dead Sea has water that's so salty, it's very easy to float in.

This woman is floating in the very salty water of the Dead Sea.

Magnets

A magnet is a piece of metal that can pull some other types of metal towards it. Magnetism is a force. It happens because of the way atoms are arranged inside the metal.

Iron filings (tiny bits of iron) stick to the parts of this horseshoe-shaped magnet where its magnetic force is strongest.

Pushing and pulling

Magnetic forces are strongest at the two ends of a magnet. These ends are called the north pole and the south pole. If you try to put two magnets' poles together, they will either stick to each other or push each other away.

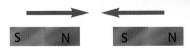

A north pole and a south pole always pull towards each other. This is called magnetic attraction.

Two poles of the same type always push each other away. This is called magnetic repulsion.

Magnetic fields

The area of force around a magnet is called its magnetic field. Our planet is magnetic and has its own magnetic field. It pulls compass needles so that they always point north.

Like all magnets, the Earth has magnetic north and south poles. They are near the North Pole and South Pole you can see on a globe.

Magnets at work

You might use magnets to stick notes on your refrigerator. They are also used inside motors, DVD players and watches. Because magnets only attract some metals, such as iron, they are also used to separate materials from each other.

Which metals?

Try testing different metal things around your house with a magnet. You will need:

a magnet; metal objects, such as pins, coins, scissors, cutlery, jewellery

Will it stick?

	Guess	Actual
Tin can	☑	☐
Coin	☑	☐
Bottle	☒	☐
Ball	☒	☐

1. Guess which objects the magnet will attract.

2. Now test them by seeing if the magnet sticks to them.

The objects the magnet sticks to probably contain some iron, steel or nickel.

This huge magnet is being used to separate different types of metal so that they can be re-used.

"Maglev" trains use magnetic repulsion to make them float just above a rail. This allows them to move very smoothly.

Internet link

For a link to a website where you can try a fun online experiment about magnets, go to **www.usborne-quicklinks.com**

Light and colour

Light is a form of energy. Most of the light on our planet comes from the Sun. Light comes from other places too – electric lights, candle flames and even some types of animals.

Lines and shadows

Light always travels in straight lines. If light hits an object that's not see-through, it can only shine past it, not around it. This makes a shadow where the light can't reach.

★ Light shines in straight lines. Shadows happen because rays of light cannot bend around objects.

Light can turn a corner if it reflects (bounces) off a surface, such as a mirror.

★ You can make light turn a corner. If you shine a lamp or torch at a mirror, the light will bounce off it.

The speed of light

When you flick a light switch, light seems to fill the room instantly. This is because light travels very fast. It moves at 300,000km (186,000 miles) per second.

It takes eight minutes for light to travel from the Sun to the Earth.

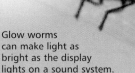

Glow worms can make light as bright as the display lights on a sound system.

Internet link

For a link to a website where there are activities to help you to find out more about colours and how they are made, go to **www.usborne-quicklinks.com**

Seeing light

We see things because our eyes are designed to collect and sense light (there's more about eyes on page 31). When we see an object, we're really seeing light reflecting off it.

We see the Moon because light from the Sun reflects off it.

Colours

Bright white light is made up of different colours of light mixed together.

We see colours because some objects only reflect one colour of light. For example, a green leaf only reflects green light, so it looks green.

A piece of shaped glass called a prism can split white light into all its colours.

White light shining into prism

Prism

Separate colours of light shining out of prism

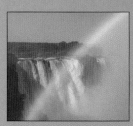

Sometimes raindrops act like mini-prisms. They split sunlight into lots of colours, making a rainbow.

Did you know?

• Most people can detect more than 10 million different shades of colour.

• Some people are "colourblind". They can see some colours, but find it hard to tell the difference between red and green.

• Many animals see only in shades of grey, not in colour.

• Scientists think it's impossible for anything in the Universe to travel faster than light.

Sound

Sound is a form of energy. It is made of vibrations (back-and-forth movements) that can move through air, solid things and liquids, but not through empty space.

Sound vibrations

When you hit a drum, speak or clap, molecules in the air vibrate. We hear sounds because the vibrations travel through air, or other substances, and hit our ears. (Read more about ears on page 31.)

The loudest sounds, such as a rocket lift-off (180 decibels), will damage your ears.

A rattlesnake can make a rattling sound with its tail to scare enemies. The movement of rings on its tail makes molecules in the air vibrate.

Loud and soft

The volume (loudness) of a sound depends on how big the vibrations are. Volume is measured in units called decibels. This chart shows how loud different sounds are in decibels.

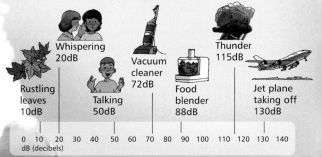

Whispering 20dB

Vacuum cleaner 72dB

Thunder 115dB

Rustling leaves 10dB

Talking 50dB

Food blender 88dB

Jet plane taking off 130dB

0 10 20 30 40 50 60 70 80 90 100 110 120 130 140
dB (decibels)

High and low

Fast sound vibrations make high sounds. Slower sound vibrations make lower sounds. The highness or lowness of a sound is called its pitch. Some animals can hear pitches we can't hear.

Internet link

For a link to a website where you can find out how to make a musical instrument and make your own sounds, go to **www.usborne-quicklinks.com**

This farmer's whistle makes a very high sound. Dogs can hear it, but people can't.

Elephants can make sounds so low that people can't hear them.

Scientists know that blue whales make the lowest, loudest sound of any animal.

Making music

Musical instruments have parts that vibrate to make sounds. When someone plays an instrument, they make different notes by changing the speed of the vibrations.

On a violin, shorter strings vibrate faster and make higher-pitched notes. Violin players make the strings shorter or longer with their fingers.

Feel sound vibrations

You can't normally feel sound vibrations in the air, but you can in this experiment. You will need:

a radio; a blown-up balloon

Turn the radio on and hold the balloon next to its speaker. The vibrations travel through the balloon and into your fingers.

Electricity

Electricity is a very useful form of energy. It can easily be changed into other forms of energy, such as light and heat. It makes lights, televisions and computers work. Most of the electricity we use comes from power stations.

Lightning is a kind of static electricity that's made when water molecules inside clouds rub together during storms.

In power stations, machines called generators turn energy from fuel, such as coal or gas, into electricity.

Cables and pylons carry electricity to transformers.

Transformers, like this one, make electricity safe for us to use.

Getting electricity

Electricity travels from power stations to homes along underground cables, or wires attached to high pylons. They are kept out of reach, because if electricity touches you, it can give you a dangerous shock.

Here, the cables go underground.

Using electricity

When an appliance, such as a toaster, is plugged in, it is connected to the electricity supply. Electricity flows into it and gives it the energy to work. Plastic does not conduct, or carry, electricity well, so it is used to cover electrical appliances. This stops you from getting a shock.

Can you guess which of these uses the most electricity in one minute?

Answer: the hairdryer

Internet link

For a link to a website where you can find out how to make electricity from a lemon, go to **www.usborne-quicklinks.com**

Static electricity

Static electricity is a form of electricity that builds up in some substances when they are rubbed together. It can make objects stick to each other. Do you ever feel a small shock when you touch metal? This is caused by a small build-up of static in your body as you move around.

Make static electricity

You will need:

a balloon; a sweater

1. Blow up a balloon, and rub it up and down on a sweater a few times.

2. Gently put the balloon on the wall. Static electricity makes it stick there.

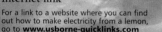

Transformer

The orange and yellow lines show the route the cables take underground.

Electricity flows from the underground cables into homes.

Computers

Computers are information machines. They can store numbers, words, pictures and other information, and process them, or make changes to them.

Internet link

For a link to a website where you can click on the parts inside a computer to find out what they do, go to **www.usborne-quicklinks.com**

How computers work

Computers contain lots of circuits. These are pathways that can carry electricity. Information travels around them very fast as a code made of electrical signals.

Monitor

Speaker

CPU

This is a modern home computer. You enter information using the keyboard and mouse, and it is displayed on the monitor. Information is processed inside the CPU or Central Processing Unit.

Keyboard

Mouse

This picture shows some of the electronic circuits inside a computer.

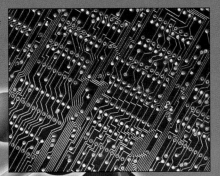

Scientists often use computers to help them make scientific pictures. This is a computer-generated image of DNA, an important molecule found in living things.

Hardware and software

Computer equipment is called hardware. To work, computers also need instructions called software. Computer programmers make software by writing sets of special instructions, called computer programs.

This picture of a mouse head was made using 3D animation software. Here you can see two of the different stages involved in creating it.

On the Internet

Computers can be linked together, or networked, so that they can share information. The Internet is a huge worldwide network that any computer can be connected to. It has lots of uses.

Information is stored on the Internet in the form of web pages. Each page is a screen full of text or pictures. Here are some examples*:

Changing the world

Since they were invented in the 1950s, computers have changed the world. They do sums much faster than humans, and make it easy to send information around the world.

Computers have helped scientists to explore space. This computer-controlled robot was sent to Mars to study its surface.

*Microsoft® Internet Explorer, Microsoft® Outlook®.

Science words

This page explains some of the words you will find in this book and other science books.

atom one of the very tiny units that everything is made of.

bacteria tiny single-celled creatures.

cartilage a material like bone, but softer and bendier.

cell a very small living unit. All living things are made up of cells.

chemical reaction a change that sometimes happens when two materials are mixed together.

contract get smaller.

density how heavy a material is for its size.

digestion the way your body breaks down food into useful chemicals.

electricity a form of energy which is used to make machines work.

endangered species a type of living thing that's in danger of dying out.

energy the power that makes things work. Heat, light, movement and electricity are all forms of energy.

equator an imaginary line around the middle of the Earth.

expand get bigger.

experiment a scientific test to find out about how something works.

force a push or a pull. Forces can make things move, stop, speed up, slow down or change shape.

friction a force that slows things down as they rub or slide against each other.

galaxy a huge group of stars.

gravity a force that pulls objects towards each other.

habitat the place where an animal or plant lives, such as a wood or a lake.

heat a form of energy which we can feel. It flows from warmer objects into cooler ones.

the Internet a worldwide network of computers that are linked together so that they can share information.

kinetic energy the kind of energy that something has when it moves.

light a form of energy that we can sense with our eyes.

magnet a piece of metal that pulls some types of metal towards it.

materials the different kinds of stuff all around us, such as water, metal, wood, glass and plastic.

Milky Way the name of the galaxy that our planet, the Earth, is part of.

molecules tiny particles made up of atoms. Everything is made of them.

moon a ball of rock that orbits around a planet.

nucleus the central, most important part of a cell or atom.

observe look at something carefully.

orbit travel around a larger object.

organ a body part, such as the heart, lungs, eyes, liver or brain.

particle a very small piece or part.

photosynthesis the way plants make food using energy from the Sun.

pitch how high or low a sound is.

planet a large ball of rock or gas that orbits around a star.

poles the parts of a magnet where its pulling power is strongest.

potential energy energy that's stored up and ready to use.

reproduce make babies. All plants, animals and other living things reproduce.

robot a machine that can make its own decisions.

science what we know about the Universe and how things work.

skeleton a framework of bones that holds you up and protects your insides.

Solar System our Sun and all the planets and moons orbiting it.

species a type of plant, animal or other living thing.

star a huge ball of very hot gas floating in space.

the Sun the star that our planet, the Earth, orbits around.

technology using science to invent machines and other useful things.

temperature how hot something is.

theory an idea about how something works or why it is the way it is.

the Universe everything that exists in space, including our world.

upthrust a pushing force that makes things float.

X-ray a kind of photograph that can show the inside of the body.

Index

Acknowledgements

The publishers are grateful to the following for permission to reproduce material:

Key
t = top, m = middle, b = bottom, l = left, r = right

Cover ©Digital Vision; ©John Russell; p1 ©Digital Vision; p3 ©Digital Vision; p4tr ©Digital Vision; p4m ©Samsung Electronics UK: The Samsung SG-A400 is another example of an innovative product from Samsung Electronics UK; p4bl ©Jorg & Petra Wegner/Bruce Coleman The Natural World; p5tr ©Mehau Kulyk/Science Photo Library; p5br ©Sam Ogden/Science Photo Library; p6 ©William Curtsinger/Science Photo Library; p7tr ©RobertHarding.com; p7br ©Roger Ressmeyer/CORBIS; p8tl ©Stockbyte; p8br ©BSIP/CHAIX/Science Photo Library; p9t ©NASA; p9t ©Digital Vision; ©Mariner 10, Astrogeology Team, U. S. Geological Survey; ©Digital Vision; p9m ©Digital Vision; p9bl ©Stockbyte; p9br ©Digital Vision; p10bl ©Digital Vision; p11tr ©Martin Bond/Science Photo Library; p11br ©Digital Vision; p12 ©Richard Hamilton Smith/CORBIS; ©Digital Vision; p14tl ©Digital Vision; p14tm ©Douglas Peebles/CORBIS; p14tr ©Digital Vision; p16tr ©Stockbyte; p16b ©Digital Vision; p17br ©Kim Taylor/Bruce Coleman The Natural World; p18tl ©Prof. P. Motta, Dept. of Anatomy, University "La Sapienza", Rome/Science Photo Library; p19tr ©Dr. Linda Stannard/UCT/Science Photo Library; p19br ©Colin Cuthbert/Science Photo Library; p21br ©Danny Lehman/CORBIS; p22tr ©Bruce Coleman/Gary Vestal; p22bl ©Bruce Davidson/Naturepl.com; p25t ©National Cancer Institute/Science Photo Library; p25b ©Lester V. Bergman/CORBIS; p26bl ©Dave Roberts/Science Photo Library; p29bl ©Juergen Berger, Max-Planck Institute/Science Photo Library; pp30-31m ©Mehau Kulyk/Science Photo Library; p31br ©Garry Gay/Alamy.com; p32b ©Digital Vision; p33tr ©BSIP, Barthelemy/Science Photo Library; p33br ©Digital Vision; p34tl ©Michael Freeman/CORBIS; p34lm ©Adrienne Hart-Davis/Science Photo Library; p34bl ©Larry Lee Photography/CORBIS; p35r ©Digital Vision; p36tr ©foodfolio/Alamy.com; p36bl ©Adrienne Hart-Davis/Science Photo Library; p37tl ©Reto.Guntli/Arcaid.co.uk; p37br ©Phil Schermeister/CORBIS; p41b ©Lowell Georgia/CORBIS; p42tr ©Digital Vision; p42b ©Alfred Pasieka/Science Photo Library; p43t ©Dave G. Houser/CORBIS; p44 ©Courtesy of NASA/JPL/Caltech; p44tr ©Mariner 10, Astrogeology Team, U. S. Geological Survey; ©USGS; p44br Courtesy of NASA/JPL/Caltech; p45 Courtesy of NASA/JPL/Caltech; p45tl ©NASA; p45ml ©Digital Vision; Courtesy of NASA/JPL/Caltech; p47 ©Hugh Sitton/Getty Images; p48m ©Brian Bailey/CORBIS; p49tr ©Digital Vision; p49br ©George D. Lepp/CORBIS; p50tr ©TEK IMAGE/Science Photo Library; p51tr ©Alex Bartel/Science Photo Library; p51b ©Transrapid International; p52ml ©Bruce Coleman Collection; p52br ©NASA; ©Digital Vision; p53tl ©Digital Vision; p53rm ©Phototake/Robert Harding Picture Library; p53br ©Digital Vision; p54tl ©Digital Vision; p54mr ©D. Robert & Lorri Franz/CORBIS; p55br ©Howard Allman; p58tr Picture supplied by Apple, Courtesy of Apple; p58bl ©Alfred Pasieka/Science Photo Library; p58br ©Digital Vision; p59t ©2001 Aardman Animations, by Dan Lane; p59mr Screen shots reprinted by permission from Microsoft Corporation; p60-61 (background) ©Digital Vision

Additional artwork: Andy Burton, Ian Jackson, Kuo Kang Chen, Guy Smith, David Wright, Christyan Fox, Michael Wheatley and Helen Wood.

Additional design, editorial and digital image manipulation contributions: Laura Parker, Keith Newell, Stephanie Jones, Nelupa Hussain, Francesca Allen, Joanne Kirkby, Georgina Hooper, John Russell and Keith Furnival.

Additional consultancy: Stuart Atkinson, Ruth King, Dr. Margaret Rostron, Dr. Kristina Routh, Dr. Tom Weston.